Mapping the In

Decoding the Symbols of Dreams and Everyday Life

By Susan Zummo

"Dreams are illustrations...from the book your soul is writing about you."
Marsha Norman, *The Fortune Teller*

With deep gratitude for all the seen and unseen help along the way.

Introduction

Dream interpretation and dream symbols have been a part of my life for as long as I can remember. From my earliest memories I had a vivid and detailed dreamscape. As a child I began each day going downstairs to meet my father at the kitchen table, and I would announce I'd had a dream. I'd tell him everything I could recollect from my night's adventures. My father always listened to me, but never commented on my dreams one way or the other. His lack of reaction encouraged the belief in me that having such vivid dreams and remembering them was natural and normal, and I continued our morning ritual well into my teenage years.

My foray into dream interpretation began with my best friend at the age of twelve. Every morning that summer, we would share our nightly dreams and interpretations. I have vivid memories of the two of us sitting in front of her house and sharing our dreams from the night before. We took turns in the telling of them and together we would decide what the dreams meant based on our young lives at the time and our own intuition. Little did we know at the time that we were learning the universal vocabulary of the soul.

Years later I started to search for dream interpretation books to discover a "dictionary" that would give me symbol meanings that felt right to me. But I was always disappointed at definitions that made no sense and I gave up on them altogether. I didn't understand at the time that the **key to interpreting any symbol depends on the experiences and beliefs of the interpreter**. Individual experiences and interpretations can vary widely from person to person. Someone who has a fear of drowning will have a very different view of a deep lake than someone who loves to fish. I call it "one person's placid lake is someone else's violent drowning." Different symbols have different meanings to each of person based on their personal history. The soul uses the language of symbols when it communicates with us via the intuition. Clairvoyants (visual intuitives) receive their information in the form of symbols and must interpret those symbols for their clients. For them, understanding the language of symbols is a must. Symbols can also come in the form of sounds, smells, etc. to be interpreted by anyone willing to look at their deeper meaning.

Dreams awaken us to different aspects of ourselves, different dimensions of reality and allow us to interact with our spirit through these unique experiences. As creators of the world we experience, everything that happens in life is a perfect reflection of our inner landscape. The soul speaks to us through our intuition with symbols. These symbols are the language the soul uses to communicate its plans and advice for us in this life. Understanding the language of your soul opens an encyclopedic source of information. This information can be used to avoid disasters, improve our lives and the lives of those we love.

What makes this book different from the rest is its personalized focus. I'm going to show you a method of dream interpretation you can use to decode your *own* symbols and life events. You can expand your own personal dream dictionary and learn how to apply symbol interpretation to every area of your life, not just dreams. Once you learn how to apply this easy process to symbol interpretation, you'll be able to create a dream dictionary that will always be right for you! You'll also learn how to recognize the different types of dream experiences that express themselves while we're asleep. Knowing the type of dream you've had provides the context in which to interpret its symbols and actions.

Setting the Stage

The Two Basic Rules of Dream Interpretation

Rule #1: There are no wrong answers. Your interpretation is the correct interpretation – always. Don't doubt and second guess yourself when interpreting dream symbols or life events. No one is going to be more right than you when it comes to your experiences and beliefs.

Rule #2: When in doubt about the meaning of the symbol, use your intuition. Trust your soul to choose symbols that will have meaning for you. Feel free to sit with a symbol and allow it to speak to you. Intuition gets stronger and clearer with practice and trust.

"Dreams are actually lessons in the Cosmic Consciousness. They come to man for a reason; the purpose is to awaken in him a realization of the dream nature of the universe and of the method of its operation." Paramahansa Yogananda, *Man's Eternal Quest*

Getting Started

Dream and Symbol Interpretation Foundations

Everything in the universe is communicating with us all the time. The soul communicates with us via the intuition utilizing the language of symbols. You can substitute the words *subconscious, reality, Universe, God, Spirit, Source* or some other word that resonates with you. Our soul is not the only communicator in our dreams, and we'll cover that later in the book.

"Much of our waking experience is but a dream in the daylight."
-George Elliott, *Impressions of Theophrastus Such*

We find dream interpretation fascinating because it provides us with hints and insights into who we are, our emotions, beliefs and desires. Some dreams can even give a look at possible futures. There is something mysterious and exciting about our nightly dream adventures. And on some level, we know that they are trying to tell us something important, whether we can grasp it or not. One way to look at dreams is that everyone and everything in the dream is a reflection of us, and if everything in a dream can represent us, why can't everything in life reflect some part of our personal inner landscape?

Dreams are not the only way for us to learn deep truths about ourselves. Consider for a moment, that the soul is not limited to communicating with us only through dreams. The soul is an unlimited aspect of the Creator and can use any type of symbol to convey a message. As an agent of Higher Awareness, it will use every available avenue of communication to reach our conscious mind. This might mean speaking to us through the everyday things in our lives, especially through our personal environment and belongings. Where we reside, our cars and our personal vehicle – our body – are all energetically linked to us, and therefore natural mediums for the soul's message.

Have you ever had the experience of getting very angry with someone and yelling at them? We all have. But have you given much thought to the possibility that burning your hand later on a hot oven rack was your soul's way of letting you know that anger and violent thoughts only come back to us in the end?

Your soul has been communicating with you from the very beginning whether you've been aware of it or not. Through the use of repeating symbols and scenarios in daily life, the soul can provide valuable lessons and information designed to assist us in accomplishing the individual purpose we were each born with. Some of these repeating symbols will occur through life events, work situations, relationships, dreams and even our environment.

Most people I meet have a personal number, a number that comes up in their life over and over. They notice it on a clock and in their home address, on license plates and in songs. These numbers seem to follow them wherever they go in life, even on birthdays and anniversaries. Knowing the meaning of specific numbers will decode the message being sent your way.

If we are willing to look and open to receive the messages given to us, we can heal our emotions, elevate our consciousness and live a more harmonious life. We have a choice to move blindly through each day, wondering why and how things could randomly happen to us, or we can choose to see meaning in everything that occurs. Approaching life as a mystery to decipher enables us to know the deeper meaning of our lives.

The soul is a subtle and gentle teacher speaking to us first through our home, then through our car and finally through our body. The first attempt to reach us will be like a whisper, soft and easy to miss. It could be something as simple as blowing a fuse or popping light bulbs every time you flip a switch. If we're not paying attention, we can miss the message entirely. After all, it costs very little to change a bulb or fuse, so it might not register that there is something more going on. It would never occur to us that our energy is out of balance, so we would replace the item and move on to the next attention-grabbing activity in front of us. After a series of popping circuit breakers and light bulbs, things would settle back to normal and we would proceed as usual.

If house events are the soul's whisper, car problems are the soul's louder "outside" voice. Not a shout but not a soft whisper either. When the soul talks out loud to us, we will find that our car needs some kind of repair. This will be a louder communication because it is more intense in cost and impact. A dead battery can leave us stranded wherever we are and having to pay to get going again. A loose wire can mean an easy fix but a bill for the diagnosis and labor. Car repairs may get our attention due to the inconvenience and cost, but are they loud enough for us to stop and look at the house repairs and connect the dots? If we are paying attention, we'll connect the two events and understand that without regulating our energy output, we are using too much energy and becoming drained and depleted. This is a clear caution from the soul not to push past our limits when it comes to taking on projects or making promises that require more than we have to give.

If we are not paying attention, we'll replace the battery, pay the mechanic and wonder why this is happening when the current battery is only 3 years old. We'll wonder why the expense had to come right at this time and may even feel a little annoyed at circumstances that required a tow or loss of work. We will, however, need to keep moving forward through life to the next attention-grabbing event. The soul will not counter our free will and it loves us unconditionally. Because of this, our soul will not stop us from carrying on unconsciously. It will allow us the experience of our choice to remain unconscious of the fact that we are the ultimate creators of our life.

After missing all the clues and taps on the shoulder from our life events, the soul will shout out to us that it is time change direction. The next communication will be loud and clear because it will occur in our body. By the time a dis-ease settles into our body, we have missed all the other previous warning signals happening all around us. We might experience a pinched nerve, issues with digestion and elimination, or lack of sleep. In this example, we won't be able to move on after a quick fix because our body just won't budge. We could be down with a cold or flat on our backs after a visit to the chiropractor. This is the blessing of life reflecting our inner landscape, because once something settles into the body, nothing is going to happen until our true self is heard and cared for. Now we are forced to rest and are able to only expend our energy in the most important areas of our life, like eating, resting and eliminating the fear that underlies all these events.

We can avoid costly and time-consuming drains on our personal resources by simply honoring our own inner rhythms and needs. Movement and rest combined with addressing stressful situations can eliminate the drain on our batteries while keeping our energy balanced and flowing. This example is just one way the outer world reflects back to us to teach us important lessons. Repetition and similarity can clue us into the greater message, but we have to be willing to look at our life as interrelated symbols telling a story about us, by us and for us.

Even though we'll talk a lot about symbols and their meanings in dreams, remember that physical structures and happenings are also subject to symbolic interpretation. By doing this, we can take advantage of every tool and approach available when it comes to living a more positive, healthy and spiritually connected life.

Let's start with the general definitions as a loose guide and then move on to specific symbols and their meanings to complete the picture.

Interpreting House Symbols

Everything we own has our energy in it. It is an extension of our thoughts, desires and beliefs. Think about it. The home you live in was chosen by you, furnished and decorated by you, and reflects your interests and world view. The house or home you find yourself in when dreaming is no different. Whether a symbol occurs in a dream or a waking state, the same rules will apply.

General House Definitions – The Home is Me

What floor am I on?

The floors or levels of a building reflect different levels within the dreamer. We all have these

20

levels within us: a subconscious suspended just below our waking awareness, a consciousness awareness that we know as "us", and a higher consciousness some call the super-ego or soul. What floor is the action taking place in the dream? That will tell you the area or level of your life being reflected back to you for consideration. Whether an event happens on the floor of a dream building or your own physical home, there will be symbolic information for us to learn.

Basic meanings of building levels:

- Upper floors of the house = higher consciousness, higher mind, super-conscious, future
- Main Floor = personality, ego, present
- Basement/lower floors (going underground) = subconscious, inner child, the past

A dream about going down a ramp or stairs to the lower level of a building is asking us to examine a belief held in the subconscious or rooted in the past. Perhaps a childhood issue, or something from a past life will be presented in a basement or underground space.

What room am I in?

In order to decode events happening in the (dream) house, look at the room's function. For example, **the kitchen** is where food is prepared and food is what nourishes us. The kitchen can be the room in which nourishment of all types, physical, emotional and mental takes place. Socializing with family and friends might be about emotional nourishment in the heart of the house. A dream taking place in the kitchen might be calling attention to the need to nourish the self. Many people **dream of**

cooking with family members. For them the kitchen is a place to nourish themselves with unconditional love. Of course, your personal experience with food or family gatherings in the kitchen will change the meaning of your personal symbol. If your past is filled with memories of having to sit at the table until the plate was empty, the kitchen would not be pleasant place to have a dream. Some other experiences involving food, such as having food withheld, being punished with food or disapproving looks from family members based on weight and food choice can also color the meaning of a dream in the kitchen.

The kitchen is also known as the heart of the house and may symbolize the physical heart. There will be other symbols or circumstances in the dream that will show if care needs to be taken with the heart. An example would be a dream in which the oven is broken or not working properly.

Example: I often dream of visiting with family and friends while a meal is being prepared in the kitchen. The kitchen is where deceased relatives and I visit one another. Usually my mom or grandma is cooking while my dad and I talk things over. Those dreams have a wonderful feeling of connection to happy memories for me and I always wake up feeling loved and safe.

If an appliance in the kitchen stops working, you want to look at what it does to determine what is being reflected back for consideration. **Appliances** with a thermostat speak to regulating emotions (staying cool, not overheating). Refrigerators, ovens, microwaves, etc., all fall into this category.

Example: If you're a person who loves morning coffee and the coffee maker breaks, your temper could be getting in the way of enjoying life.

The bedroom is where rest and intimacy take place depending upon your perspective. If you see the bedroom as a place for sleep, you may need more rest or 'down-time.' If the bedroom is a place of intimacy, relationship with different aspects of self or spouse/partner should be examined. Dreams of sex with someone other than your spouse or some unknown person are common and are usually about connecting with a neglected part of self. Of course, they can also be an indication of a lack of intimacy in life. The true meaning would depend on how you feel about sex and what the other person symbolically represents to you.

Example: A client reported dreaming about having sex with a co-worker. My client wasn't particularly attracted to her co-worker and wanted to know what the dream could mean. The first question I asked was, how would you describe this person? What are their personality traits? She described this individual as honest. He usually went along with the boss's ideas and tried to get along with everyone. She stated that the person had good ideas but would seek out others to work with for implementation. A follower rather than a leader. She admitted that she wasn't all that impressed with his approach to business relationships and they didn't agree on how to get things done. However, in the dream she really enjoyed the intimacy they shared.

We determined that good physical intimacy was not missing from her waking life. We decided to look at how this person was someone very different from her. My client was a go-getter, rather forceful in her business relationships and definitely a take-charge personality. She wanted to be successful in her career and get ahead. The dream asked her to take in (become intimate with) the qualities represented by this individual on a deep level. It was letting her know that there was something missing for a balanced approach to her work relationships. By becoming intimate with the dream lover's qualities, she could work better with others and share success with a team. A softer more balanced approach to projects would make her a much better candidate to move up in the company and lead teams of her own.

Children's rooms represent them and will give an indication of what is happening with their inner landscape. Observe young children when they are in their room to see where they go to play or sleep. Do they gravitate to the corners of the room or pull everything into the center?

Those in the corner are more introverted while those in the center of the room tend to be more extroverted or willful. Do they play on the bed or on the floor? (comfort versus expansion)

If your dream takes place in your child's bedroom, then you'll want to pay attention to how old the child is in the dream. Sometimes we long to go back to time when they were small and the relationship was simple and easier. In that case, the dream is a reminder of the relationship's foundation of love and acceptance. If you dream of an adult child living in their first bedroom, it can alert you to immature behavior or a childhood cause for something happening now.

Older children and teenagers' rooms are a clear indication of the confusion and emotional upheaval going on inside them. Everyone who has lived with the chaos of a teenager's bedroom knows that their inner landscape is fraught with tumultuous hormones, thoughts and ·emotions. It's always best to help your teenager organize their inner landscape rather than focus on a clean the room. Sometimes pointing out this very fact to a young adult will allow them to see how the outer mess reflects their inner chaos. Teens know that the state of their bedroom is not important; their emotional state is. Help your young adult get a handle on their emotions and the room will get cleaned.

The bathroom is where we eliminate toxins from our bodies. We may be purging feelings, thoughts and experiences that are poison to our system. This could also be a place where our parent's approach to potty training set up fear or resentment or a feeling of disappointing others at an early age. Bathroom dreams are usually connected to physical imbalance in the body due to toxic relationships, emotions or beliefs.

Example: Everyone has dreamed of going to the bathroom or needing to go at some time or another. This is most likely a cue to release toxic feelings or beliefs from your system (or even toxic persons). Elimination occurs daily, so the toxins to be released will be stresses from the day or current events. Flushing minor frustrations from your system will prevent buildup of toxic emotions and prevent larger problems later on.

Anytime a room has a **closed door** it will symbolize hidden knowledge or secrets; whether in the dreamscape or outer living environment. Closed doors can highlight areas in your life you are reluctant to address. They can be literal or figurative rooms such as a spare room that is piled up with old things waiting to be cleaned out. Another interpretation for a closed door is one of hidden knowledge waiting for you to discover. Many times, I've dreamed of walking down a hallway with closed doors on either side only to find a wise teacher waiting for me as soon as I step through a doorway.

Your past experiences are going to have more meaning and impact than the general definitions given here. Trust your intuition to provide the correct meaning for you, and pay attention to trends or patterns that emerge from your dreams over time.

The Rest of the House

Before leaving the house and looking at car symbols, there are a few more symbols I want to touch upon. For example, the **hot water heater or furnace** regulates heat (coffee pot or refrigerator) and indicates unresolved anger. **Refrigerators or freezers** refer to the need to cool down or preserve what you've gained. These symbols will help you decode life events as well as your dreams.

Electricity represents the energy flow in your home and the nervous system of the body. Problems with electrical systems will describe the fluctuations of energy within your own system. This can be physical energy or spiritual/healing energy. Be aware of the room in which the electrical problems occur for clues into what the meaning may be for your personal growth. Electrical shorts in a wall socket or a series of popping light bulbs in the living room are a buildup of energy that has no outlet for expression. The living room is where we meet in community with others. Electric issues there indicate you should share your energy with family, friends and acquaintances in a positive way.

Water represents emotion or spiritual energy. So, leaks in the roof would mean a high spiritual energy (coming from above or the upper floor) attempting to come into the home. If the people in the home are not open or able to sustain the energy, it must find its way in through cracks in the shell (roof of the house). Leaky basements point to unconscious past emotional issues trying to come to conscious awareness. Something is percolating up from the past that needs to be dealt with and healed. Once a roof leaks, it is practically impossible to permanently fix it until the inner spiritual blocks are removed. The same is true for basements or foundations that constantly flood. Something is trying to get your attention and it is *not* the house! Once the emotional issues from the past are healed, the fix for the building will be permanent or a move to another home is an option.

Dreams of drowning can also be past life memories floating to consciousness, or can mean drowning in strong emotions.

A Final Note About House Symbols

Dreaming about a childhood home or a previous house will help put a time frame around the lesson being taught. In other words, if you are dreaming about a childhood home, then the fear or talent symbolized in the dream is rooted in that period of your life. You will want to recall what was going on in your life at that time.

Example: Many times, as a young adult, I would dream of being back in the house I lived in from ages 7-14. My bedroom was where I learned about spiritual forces, hypnosis, out of body experiences and metaphysics. Dreams of being in that house are always a signal that some spiritual learning is being given to me. If the dream occurred during a time of intense self-growth, I knew I was on the verge of a positive change and step up in consciousness. At other times in my life, going back to my room was a call to return to my spiritual foundation and connect with my higher mind.

These dreams occurred at times when I was completely focused on advancing in my career or bogged down in worries about family or finances. Going back and connecting with my spiritual roots would remind me of the big picture and give me a renewed sense of spiritual purpose. I was always able to take my eyes off the ground in front of me and get an expanded view of my circumstances. Of course, shifting my focus from worry and fear to a fresh outlook and positive approach was just what I needed to move forward towards my goals. It's important to put dreams in the proper context of life's events. Intuition and a broad view of circumstances will help you determine which interpretation of a dream is most accurate.

"In dreams, we enter a world that's entirely our own."
-J.K. Rowling, *Harry Potter and the Prisoner of Azkaban*

Dreams of being in someone else's house:

There are other times when you'll be taken to the home of teacher or some other archetypal figure for instruction. I call this **"night school."** In these dreams, the house represents a place of higher learning. These structures always appear in my dreams as wooden or log homes. The walls are wood paneled and the beams are exposed for me to see the dark and light woods used in the construction. The floors are made of wood tiles and the colors are warm and rich in texture. Once I have the opportunity to become aware of the significance of the dream, I can be a full participant in the teaching. My dream recall is enhanced and the information I bring to wakefulness is always important and enlightening.

If you dream of being in the house of someone you know, you'll want to look at their overall influence in your life. The person who owns the house has now or did have a huge impact on your life. The room in which the dream takes place will give you a hint as to the type of influence and whether or not it was positive or negative.

Example: If you dream of being in a friend's home and food is being prepared, then the relationship is nurturing and beneficial to you. If, however, you don't like the food or there is a disagreement taking place at the same time, the dream is telling you that something is not matching up. The person may appear to be nurturing and supportive, but there is something that doesn't feel right about it to you. Perhaps the other person's motive is not pure or they are asking you to look at something within self that you don't want to see at this time.

Dreams of a house that you've never seen before are interesting and more common than you might think. The dream house can represent the spiritual body you are building or reflect your spiritual progress. In those dreams you will want to be aware of the type of home (A-frame, wrap around porch, multi-level, wood vs brick, etc.) and the landscaping around the home. If there are gardens or flowers around the home it is a good sign of a strong spiritual nature. The design and décor of the house may also let you know what past life influences are coming into play now (oriental furniture, Victorian décor, etc.). A Victorian style home with Oriental decor shows you bringing forth knowledge and skills from past lives. Dreams of a well-kept home in a natural setting will bring forward your natural spiritual talents and gifts. If you feel peaceful or comfortable in this setting, you'll know you're on the right path of learning.

Other times the house will represent your physical body. The upper floors are the head, the middle floors are the trunk, and the basement is the lower section and legs. Dreams of being in the upstairs bedroom while arguing with someone could provide the cause of headaches. Anger at self or another may be the underlying reason for stress headaches. Forgiveness of self and resolving the issue with the other person may be the prescription your inner self is recommending as a cure.

Keeping a dream journal and identifying the different types of homes you dream about will help you to understand what the dream is trying to teach you on a spiritual and personal level. Recognizing the type of home and its setting will alert you to the message of the dream.

Dreams of new construction or renovations are new beginnings in life. They grow out of inner changes and new outlooks. They are very positive and should encourage you to forge ahead on your current path.

Write Your House Symbols and Their Possible Meanings:

Cars – The Car is Me

"All that we see or seem is but a dream within a dream."
Edgar Allan Poe, *A Dream Within a Dream*

Our cars, like our bodies, take us where we need to go in the world. They are literally the vehicle that conveys us from one destination to another. Therefore, cars speak about our ability to move through life and the environment we live in. It's easy to see how the car can be a symbol for the body when you think about how we identify with our cars. We name them and take great care to make sure they will be a perfect match for us before taking them home. For the sake of symbol interpretation, the same definitions would apply to SUV's, trucks and vans.

Dreams of driving from one place to another refer to transitions in life. Perhaps a move from one job to another or a change in career or personal relationship. Where are you going, who is driving, is it day or night? The answers to those questions will provide added insight into the dream's message. Remember, driving in a car is about the process of change and transition. They can take us to new and exciting places we've never been before.

Some Basic Car Symbols:

- Right side of car = a man or masculine energy
- Left side of car = a woman or feminine energy
- Front of car = future events, where you are heading
- Rear of car = past or past life events

Example: An accident which impacts the left rear bumper of the car calls our attention to an issue in the past with a female.

Destination:

- A place you've never been to before – a new beginning or project in the future
- A place in the past – lessons from that period of time are impacting your present
- Work – self-esteem, your finances, new projects, daily interactions with co-workers
- Current home – you in the now – see dream symbols for the house
- College, University, Auditorium – places of higher learning – spiritual/self-growth
- Obstacles in the road - detours, blocks – fears and doubts in symbolic form

Who is driving:

- You – taking control of the situation, you are driving events through your will or actions
- Another – someone else making decisions, not in control of where you are going

Riding a bicycle vs. driving a car: Riding a bicycle means you are driving events (as opposed an engine powered vehicle). More personal effort is required to move the vehicle in any direction. When the bike turns into a boat or car to navigate the environment, it is help and support from unseen helpers.

Example: I remember a dream in which I was driving along a road on my way to school and didn't want to be late for class. At one point the road began to climb a steep hill with tight curves. As I became concerned about getting through the small roadway, the car morphed into a bicycle that I could easily maneuver. The bicycle again changed into a boat when I reached a swift river and I paddled the boat until the river ended at the base of a steep hill. The boat morphed into a bicycle once more and then switched back into a car when I reached the school. From this dream I knew that I would have the mental flexibility and tools needed for a seamless move across country. I also knew that the move would be an expansion of my spiritual growth (going up a steep hill = climbing the mountain of enlightenment).

Interpreting car symbols is easily done if you **consider the function** of the different parts of the car. Your intuition will provide you with an accurate picture of how symbols or events relate to your personal circumstances. As an example, **the windshield** of the car functions as a window to the outer world. A crack in the windshield would inhibit the ability to see clearly ahead. This lets us know that we are not seeing our circumstances accurately. Perhaps we are blocking some truth from our awareness. When our attention is not correctly focused, missteps and accidents can take place.

Some general meanings of car parts:

- Engine – the heart
- Transmission – ability to change or shift gears
- Starter – inability to get moving or start in a new direction
- Wires/electrical system – nervous system, spiritual energy flow
- Windshield wipers – remove obstacles so we can see the truth
- Tires – the legs and feet, the values we stand for

Symbolic language of car accidents:

- Hit on the right side of the car – emotional challenge with a male or issue on the right side of the body
- Hit on the left side of the car – emotional challenge with a woman or issue on the left side of the body
- Rear-end collision – emotional problem from the past needs to be immediately addressed before it escalates into greater problems in life
- Head-on collision – Stop. Change the direction of your life immediately. You are heading in the wrong direction.

Example: A fender bender on the back-left corner of the car might be a call to resolve old emotional hurts with a female in your life or to resolve any conflict with or injuries to your feminine side.

Anyone who's ever been in an accident knows that integrity and trust on the part of both parties are a must to get through a difficult time. Each person has the choice to create a healing or horror for themselves and the others involved. Pay attention to what the symbols are telling you and act accordingly for the best result for all concerned.

In my healing practice, I've worked with people who've had injuries resulting from car accidents. Without exception, those who had the most severe injuries always told me the same truth. Prior to the accident that caused their disability, a series of minor accidents took place within close proximity of one another. Looking back, each person stated that they had been forewarned but had ignored or dismissed the signals given. Remember warnings can come in the form of symbolic dreams or life events. We should be aware and heed all the information presented to us.

My personal experience interpreting accident symbols has shown me that the event holds a message and lesson for the owner of the car, not the driver. However, there is a connection between the two of you worth looking into. Here the Law of Cause and Effect (Karma) has provided an opportunity for balancing to take place between the driver and the owner. It would be in everyone's best interest to move through the process with grace and with an absence of anger. An accident in your spouse's car (whether in a dream or waking life) asks you to examine your relationship. If you are hit on the right side, it could be calling your attention to how the masculine responsibilities are portioned out in the home. At the very least, it will indicate imbalance in the relationship.

Example: Some time before we divorced, my ex was driving my car to pick up some lumber for a project. The lumber shifted and cracked the windshield. I took that to mean he wasn't seeing what needed to change in our relationship. Then the window handle on the passenger's side of my car fell off and the glove compartment door also fell off. In both cases I was not driving so I assumed they had nothing to do with me. After we separated, I bought a used Ford Omni in perfect working condition. Within the first week, the windshield cracked, the window handle and the glove box door pulled off. I couldn't have received a more direct message! I had to shift my focus from what my ex-husband had done to my life and open my eyes to what I wasn't seeing in myself. It taught me to pay attention to life events in a way I hadn't before.

Record Your Car Symbols and Their Possible Meanings:

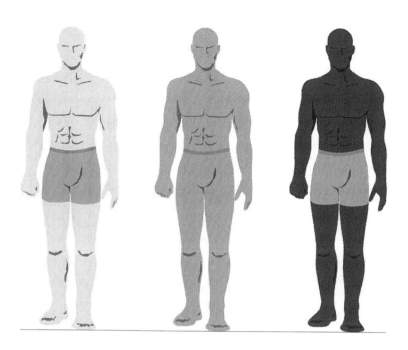

The Body – The Body is Me

Our body also speaks to us in the universal language of symbols whether we are in a dream or waking state. Everything that happens in the physical body carries an emotional teaching. The emotional and physical bodies are interdependent and interrelated. The law of cause and effect is at work whether we are aware or it or not. Science continues to prove this with new studies and findings every day.

Dreams with health warnings are more frequent than you might think. Years ago, one of my students reported dreams about losing her hair. She knew this was one common symptom of thyroid disease which was later diagnosed. Paying attention to dream experiences can provide clues to what is happening in the body.

Dreams about changing clothes can mean changing occupations or preparing for a change in life. My daughter told me of a dream she had in which she accompanied me while I shopped for new shoes. This dream took place right after she told me I was about to become a grandmother. Her dream was letting her know that my role in her life was about to change (from mother to grandmother).

The people in your dreams can be from the present, the past or past lives. They represent unresolved issues that need forgiveness, love and healing. They can even be people you will meet in the future. People in your dreams can also be spiritual teachers or loved ones who have already crossed over.

"Our truest life is when we are in dreams awake."
Henry David Thoreau, *A Week on the Concord and Merrimack Rivers*

If **everyone in the dream is you**, then everyone represents some aspect of your personality. This can happen when the person in the dream doesn't look like the Mary you know, but in the dream, you know it's Mary just the same. In this case, the subconscious is signaling you not to take Mary's appearance in your dream at face value. Mary could represent some aspect of yourself that you identify with in the other person. If you know Mary is a fearful person, the dream would be signaling you that there is fear within you that needs healing. There may be a past life connection with Mary and karma between the two of you based on the circumstances shown in the dream.

Decoding Body Symbols:

As we did with the house and car, let's look at the body holistically. Then we can see how each part functions within the whole. Remember, the purpose of this book is not to provide a list of symbols and their definitions. It's to give you a method for decoding the symbols in your own dreams and life. Always ask what the body part (or symbol) means to you. There are no wrong answers, only your answers. Your interpretation will be more accurate than mine or any other expert because the event or symbol is personal to you and your experiences. For example, female breasts represent motherhood and nourishment from the mother aspect. They can also represent sexual attraction. These are very different feelings about the same part of the body. Each interpretation will completely change the message in the life event or dream.

Symbolic meaning of the body:

- Front of the body – what you show to the world
- Back of the body – the past, something hidden
- Internal organs – your current state as a result of the accumulations of the past
- Right side of the body – masculine or male
- Left side of the body – feminine or female

General symbols based on body function:

- Mind or Head – thought patterns, self-talk about who we are and our beliefs
- Feet – our foundation – what we stand on (can mean principles)
- Legs – move us forward, fears about change and movement
- Heart – emotional pain, betrayal and hurt feelings, your capacity to love self and other
- Shoulders – where we carry our feelings of being responsible for others
- Hands – the ability to grasp life and make it work for you

Organs of the body:

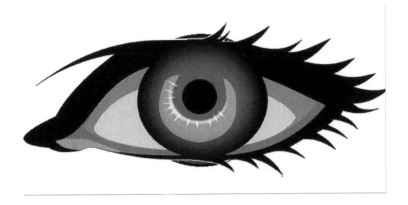

Eyes: like windshields or windows – seeing clearly or not seeing the bigger picture

Liver: anger at self, feeling like a victim, helplessness, over-identifying with the suffering of others

Pancreas: inability to feel love from others

Gall bladder: poor self-image about how the physical body looks, indulging in gossip

Intestines: ability to assimilate new ideas and release old beliefs

Ears: are all about hearing the truth. Look at the age of person involved. Children hear everything that goes on around them.

Chronic ear infections in young children indicate they are disturbed by things they hear at home. Rather than say, *"when you two fight it upsets me,"* they get ear infections to block out the anger and fear. **Hearing loss** in older adults is a way of blocking out the rest of the world whose message has become unfamiliar and changing too quickly. Loss of hearing effectively allows the person to become focused on their own inner landscape to the exclusion of the outer world. This can happen to persons of any age who are afraid or unwilling to move forward or take in the changes in the world around them.

Lungs: take in life-sustaining breath; our soul comes into our body on the breath. Smoking and congestion in the lungs block us from living a spiritual and healthy life. Congestion in the head or lungs is a red flag that the body is trying to get something out of its system. Your body will surround the anger with mucous or other tissue and then attempt to expel it as a way of removing it from the body. **Congestion in the lungs** would refer to pain and hurt over past emotional wounds. **Congestion in the head** alerts us to the physical impact of angry thoughts about the self or others.

Digestive System:

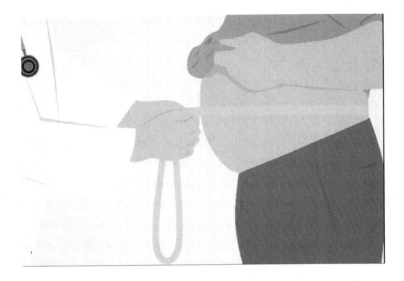

Fear and frustration manifest in the stomach. They lead to ulcers and gastronomic ailments, especially when we try to control others or manipulate circumstances to produce an outcome we want. It doesn't matter if you are trying to protect a loved one from making a mistake or bad decision. Whenever we are motivated by fear, **the stomach and solar plexus** will be called into play. If in a dream you are feeling hunger or pain in the stomach, think about where you are experiencing fear or a lack in your life. If your physical body is experiencing stomach issues, it indicates a pattern of fear or anxiety that is constantly running through your system. Minor stomach issues should not be ignored, as they can turn into chronic, debilitating problems that can negatively impact the quality of your life.

Intestines: This part of the body is about eliminating that which we no longer need. Emotional pains show up in these organs as well as the heart. Rigid thinking from the mind impacts this area of the body as well. Holding your metaphorical breath, not wanting to move or rock the boat, will cause constipation in the body as we try to hold on unnecessarily to people or situations. Letting go of the need to keep a tight hold on life, on all levels, is the key to relief.

Stress related ailments will have multiple symbolic events or symptoms attached to them. Years of physical neglect, poor habits and increasing stress will eventually break down your natural immunity. **Chronic heart disease** may follow a lifetime of strained relationships and love. I was not surprised that my father needed quadruple bypass surgery after years of family betrayals.

My clients are surprised to find that I am able to decode their emotional challenges based only on what's happening in their bodies. When someone comes to me in emotional distress, I know to look for stomach problems, congestion in the lungs and auto-immune issues. We can address the emotional cause while health care providers work on the physical. Decoding body symbols tells you everything about a person without invading their privacy.

Your body is the last line of defense in your well-being. If something is happening to your body in the dream or waking state, you will want to address it immediately. Once dis-ease settles into the physical body, we have no choice but to deal with what has taken root. We cannot afford to ignore the body when it breaks down even if we have managed to avoid looking at all the signs. We must stop everything to heal the body or we cannot move forward and experience the life we want and deserve.

Example: A student reported her oil burner had stopped working overnight and her house had no heat one particularly cold January. She had called a repairman to come out and he was able to get it working again by replacing the valve in the unit. Sometime later the same student shared that the car she drove had to have the engine replaced as it was old and had blown a gasket. She confessed to me that she had not kept up with regular service checks but found a good mechanic to get it back on the road for a reasonable price.

I was saddened, but not surprised, to learn some months later that her husband had suffered a heart attack. As it turned out the car she drove was in his name and he had been avoiding doctors and self-care for many years. As her experiences indicated, there was a small cost and inconvenience when the event took place in the house. Both cost and inconvenience increased with the car repair and reached maximum impact with her husband's heart attack. At that point lifestyle and emotional changes had to take place and could no longer be ignored.

Record Your Body Symbols and Their Possible Meanings:

Types of Dreams in the Inner Landscape:

Precognitive Dreams

Precognitive dreams are meant to alert us to future situations so we can be prepared to deal with them effectively. In general, precognitive dreams feel like you have had a real experience, not a dreaming experience. It is often difficult to realize that you were asleep and dreaming upon waking from a precognitive dream. The quality of the experience is such that you are left with a clear knowing that the dream events have already happened. It will feel as if you are remembering a memory rather than recalling a dream. Ask your intuition if a dream is a literal prediction or a foreshadowing of events based on current trends. Intuition will also help interpret dream symbols to determine the correct action.

Perhaps the most famous precognitive dreamers were the wives of Julius Caesar and Pontius Pilate. They both dreamed of impending disaster for their respective spouses. As a young person I remember reading many accounts of people who dreamed of President John F. Kennedy's assassination before he went to Dallas. Often, we hear predictive dreams surrounding public figures or events after the fact. After 9/11 numerous people came forward with stories of their dreams foretelling the events of that day.

The Bible also refers to precognitive dreams like Pharaoh's dream of 7 fat and 7 thin cattle. Joseph decoded it as referring to seven years of abundance followed by seven years of famine – a warning of future events.

Example: Many of us know someone who had a precognitive dream that involved seeing a loved one before making their transition. I had a visit from my aunt in a dream before she died in which she was pain free and with my grandmother and father. In the dream I spoke to her and knew that all was well. Her passing was less traumatic for me knowing that she was in good company and feeling free again.

Although potentially disturbing, these dreams can help us to emotionally prepare for a loved one's passing. Contemplating the death of a loved one is never a comfortable feeling, but meeting them in a dream can be part of a healthy grieving process. Often the dream visit brings a sense of peace, closure and acceptance.

Knowing that something unpleasant is ahead may not necessarily be terrible. Bad weather or cancelled flight alerts may not bring a smile to your face, but they will allow you to make alternate plans. This will save time, money and even your life.

Not all dreams that a loved one is dying are precognitive in nature. They can provide an opportunity to address and resolve fears connected around death. They can also alert us to something going on in our loved one's life that we are feeling on an intuitive level. It can be a chance to experience how we would feel if that person died before we reconciled or had that talk. This can prompt us to take action and heal situations before it's too late.

Of course, many positive dreams are precognitive and can help us more smoothly navigate daily life.

"Dreams are today's answers to tomorrow's questions."
Edgar Cayce

Example: One of my students told me that she dreamed an entire job interview the night before it occurred. In the dream she was sitting before a young woman and answering all the interview questions with confidence. The dream interviewer hired my student on the spot. When interviewed the next day, the personnel manager asked her the same questions as in her dream! Naturally the interview was a success. She already had a dream practice run and remembered all the right answers for the interview.

Example: In 2001 another student had a dream of standing in the driveway of a house he and his father built together. They were working in construction at the time. In the dream the owner had offered him the opportunity to buy it at a great price. He was excited about the dream because he always wanted to buy a home of his own but couldn't afford it at the time. Several months later my student actually was in the driveway of this particular home doing some maintenance work for the owner. His dad pulled up and asked if he wanted to buy the home for the balance on the owner's loan. It seems the owner needed to relocate for work and was in a hurry to sell. My student and his dad bought the home and it began a healing process for the two of them.

Inter-dimensional dreams

The Upanishads speak of three worlds. One is *here*, our waking world, another is the heavens, *over there*, and the third is *the bridge* in between, our dream world. On the bridge of the dream world we can meet others from over there and also learn to travel there ourselves. In dreams we can cross dimensions and visit realms that are more difficult to reach in the waking state. This is because the conscious mind is relaxed enough to be submissive to the spiritual self. We have the ability to traverse dimensions during the dream state when the mind is fluid and the body is relaxed. Lucid dreaming and certain dream symbols offer us a gateway to other dimensions that we would not normally have access to. With enough attention and *in*tention, we can easily practice moving from one dimension to another in the dream state at will.

No doubt you've already made dimensional shifts in the dream state and weren't aware of it. You may have simply interpreted these experiences as strange or unusual dreams and never given them a second thought.

In order to recognize an inter-dimensional dream, pay attention to the details and feelings in the dream. In normal dreams, the events and symbols will fit in a way that makes sense in the dream and in real life. For example, if you dream about being in a house, you expect the bedrooms to be consistent with the style of the home. Cars will run as expected. Even though the landscape won't necessarily have the look and feel of daily life, it won't appear alien either.

Inter-dimensional dreams will have a "slightly off" undercurrent running in the background. In the dream you will become aware of something out of sync with the environment. Your mind will try to make the scene fit or call your attention to some discrepancy in the hopes of resolving it. You may notice the landscape and all the buildings are a variation of the same color. You may notice windows along a hallway in a house where pictures would normally be. You may see a microwave being used as a refrigerator. The color of the trees or landscape will appear foreign and structures will not fit with the locale. While you may feel you are in Egypt, all the pyramids are made of glass and steel. Colors will be more vibrant and the angles in the landscape may be sharper.

Sometimes the people in the dream are the clue that you've traveled between dimensions. Their clothing (a physician wearing overalls) or their appearance (no eyebrows) may be a subtle a sign of dimensional travel. At other times the signs can be so subtle that you don't even realize it was an inter-dimensional dream until after you've woken up. No matter what the signal, you'll know because your mind would've been chewing on it throughout the dream. Your mind will try to make a strange scene look normal so you are not frightened by it.

Your mind is always trying to make sense of what you're seeing. It will make sure your encounter is "normal" even if that means creating an inconsistent scenario. Of course, the mind also likes to be in control. It will interpret what it sees into a language of dream pictures that approximate "normal". Some alien landscapes are so far out of our normal range that the mind substitutes something more recognizable. Exposure to foreign environments and alien landscapes through movies and other media expands your mind's ability to work with what might otherwise be frightening. The mind doesn't know what is real and what is not. Exposing your mind to different images gives it a language to interact with strange scenarios.

"Dreaming is an advanced evolutionary exercise, a way the brain can go on an extended journey into that other reality."
Robert T. Bakker, *Raptor Red*

Example: One of the worlds I traveled to for a period of time was all orange red – the colors of brick and clay. The sky was always filled with shades of red, burnt orange and rusty brick colors. The buildings were made of red clay and redwood. The ground was made of red dusty dirt and there was no vegetation that I could see. Each time I turned up there, I had a specific task and amount of time to complete that task. It was not a place I enjoyed visiting but was rather a place of assigned work. There was always a serious feeling and the pressure of getting things done quickly. No one ever smiled, and I never felt anything positive about the place … only a sense of accomplishment when the task was done. I've never missed going there.

Dreams which act as gateways to other dimensions have "doorways" built into them. These doorways may present themselves as stairwells in buildings, escalators, or actual doors. Sometimes they can even appear as bicycles or small cars. Regardless of how the gateway presents itself, you will be required to exert your will to pass through these bridges.

There is a sensation of purpose in the dream. If you aren't paying attention you may suddenly find yourself in a strange or "wrong" place for the dream. Then you may spend the rest of the dream trying to get back to where you began. It can be frustrating and difficult to find the dream doorway if you don't know a dimensional crossing took place. More often than not, you will eventually wake up with a feeling of frustration for not being able to get where you wanted to go. Once you become aware of your dream doorways, you will be able to shift dimensions with awareness. Being aware in a dream, otherwise known as lucid dreaming, allows you to fully participate in the dream. Lucid dreaming lets you bring experiences and teachings back to the waking state.

Example: Doorways in my dreams are presented as stairwells in buildings that go up. My dream can begin with me walking down a street in a rural town or busy city. At some point I will enter a modern office building and walk up the stairwell to a metal door with a small window. Many times, I exit the door into a hospital-type setting and am asked to do healing on those in the ward. Unlike normal hospital wards, these rooms have no furniture. People are sleeping on the floor or sitting in chairs waiting for their treatments. One of my most memorable experiences was being sent into a special nursery to feed and rock the babies.

Example: A close friend of mine always had her dimensional doorways presented as escalators in the Mall of America. Upon entering the mall, she would take an escalator to the upper floors. For her, each store in the mall led to a unique place where she would receive instruction from expert teachers. Sometimes there would be a guide waiting to point her to the store she needed to visit. Other times she would be free to wander the different levels and look in different department stores. She always enjoyed her trips and would come back with a list of new tools to work with or locate in the waking world.

Warning Dreams

Warning dreams are designed to wiggle your antennae so you will be alert to certain people or life situations. They can be straight forward where an individual tells you their truth or a direct statement from your soul. Sometimes you will physically hear the words while you are dreaming. They will be direct and unmistakable and can be completely unrelated to the dream you are having. I call them "the pause for an important message".

Examples: "It's time to move" or "Don't work with that person" or "Mary can't be trusted". They may say, "Forgive your mother now" or "Look for work in another state" or "Release your anger with John." I recall one dream in particular in which I was having an uneventful experience when the stage went dark and a young blond-haired man appeared in a spotlight. In a clear voice of authority, he said, "Pay attention now. This is the lesson of the dream." He then proceeded to tell me exactly what I was supposed to learn before my alarm clock went off.

Example: Years ago, I was looking for a spiritual mentor. I found a man who advertised a one-on-one program to elevate my consciousness and clear out emotional blocks. It was just what I was looking for so I set the appointment for our first session with a sense of anticipation. The night before we were supposed to meet, I had a dream. In the dream I was standing in my kitchen telling him I probably shouldn't be working with him and that it would not turn out well for either of us. In spite of my dream, I went to the session. At that time in my life, I was too polite to cancel at the last minute. When I arrived, he instructed me to get undressed, put on a diaper and suck my thumb in front of him. I promptly left but it took months for me to recover from the fallout. His wife was a business acquaintance and attempted to ruin my reputation based on his recounting of events. Clearly, I should have heeded the warning in my dream.

Staged dreams

One of my favorite scenes in the movie The Matrix takes place when Neo is plugged into the construct program. Here Morpheus will teach and test Neo's mind on certain skills. I believe this happens to us more often than we may think. In these scenarios the soul is Morpheus and we are Neo. These dreams will feel just a little bit fake, like you are in a play or on a stage. If you find yourself in a dangerous place, you may act as if there is real peril, but inwardly know that you are just going through the motions. If you examine your feelings, there is no real danger. Other key players in these dreams may look like someone you know, but you're aware it's not them. They may look like a stranger even though you know who it is.

These dream scenarios are staged tests to give you the chance to gauge your progress on an issue. They make us aware of areas within that need to be addressed to grow spiritually. In the dream state you will always act and react as your true self, not the façade the world sees or who you'd like to think you are. When a scene is set up for you, you act from of your true inner self. Dreaming of ex-spouses or partners will give you a chance to see if you are still carrying any anger or hurt feelings from the past relationship.

"In dreams no man wears a mask."
-Edward Counsel, *Maxims*

Example: At times, I've had dreams where I would be placed in a situation and observed to monitor my personal spiritual growth. A dream that stands out took place in a house to which my spiritual teacher escorted me. The house was made of white wood. White is the color of spirituality and places of higher learning are always made of wood for me. My escort led me upstairs to higher realms of consciousness through a staircase bridge. He opened a particular door off the winding hallway and I stepped through. I assumed we were entering the room together. As soon as I crossed the threshold my guide pulled the door closed and locked me in. I opened the door opposite me and stepped into that room only to be confronted by an image of the devil himself. He was ten feet tall, red, horned, with cloven feet and a forked tail, and he was slavering over me. I could feel his breath on my face. In the dream I thought, "wow, you just can't get around archetypes." This was my mind trying to cope with the scene before it. Even though I knew this was just a representation and not 'real', my body was shaking with fear and I was scared out my wits. The fear I was feeling was quite real to me in the dream state. I was petrified with it. In the dream, I took a deep breath, faced this devil and began to say, "I am the Light" with a quaking voice and continued to repeat it until I was calm and unafraid. I knew I had passed the test by standing my ground and asserting my belief in the power of Light over darkness. The beast transformed into a beautiful male being who smiled kindly at me. I turned around and went back through the unlocked door into the hall. Upon awakening, I understood that I was walking my truth and not just giving it lip service. My unguarded reactions and actions allowed me to pass the test – I was walking my talk.

Night School, Night Shift

I refer to dreams where spiritual growth and esoteric instruction are given as **Night School.** These are the dreams you have of being in a classroom or auditorium with a group of people you may or may not know. The teaching will make perfect sense in the dream and you may even get to practice before waking up. If you can remember the details upon awakening, I recommend recording them immediately. The information may be the answer to a personal question or provide knowledge that will advance your service to others. You may get new healing methods, ancient knowledge of energy work or symbols that unlock vaults of information from prior lives. Some persons receive all their spiritual instruction in the dream state.

There may be personal instruction and specific initiations to awaken new skills in the dreamer. The details are brought back to waking life to help them accomplish their task of healing and transforming the world.

If you are unable to remember the teaching given in these dreams, don't fret. The teaching remains in the subconscious until it is time to be brought into the conscious mind. Consistent dream journaling improves your ability to bring the information back to the waking state.

Example: I've had students report that they were in a class with me and I was giving them new instruction or personal advice. This could be an aspect of my spirit doing the teaching. It is more likely one of their unseen teachers wearing a Susan costume to impart knowledge. On the other hand, I've personally experienced being in an auditorium with friends receiving instruction from the same teacher. We even confirmed this is a shared experience upon awakening. In those dreams I have no doubt that my teacher was providing the instruction, not a stand in. Intuition will let you know if you have had an experience with your Spirit in disguise or another type of being.

Night Shift is term I use to refer to those dream experiences where we go to do service work for others. In the section on dimensional dreaming I mentioned going to the hospital to do healing work. This is an example of Night Shift dreaming. Other examples are working with a group of people you may or may not know, usually in a foreign place. Many times, you will see familiar faces in the dream but may have never met your co-workers in waking life. I believe that we are sent to areas of the planet and places in the universe that are in need of healing and light. I don't always remember my night shift dreams but I can always tell I've been 'out doing service' based on how the dream ends. In these dreams there is a group of us preparing a meal together in a kitchen located on the third story of a house. We are cooking, washing and drying dishes and interacting with great camaraderie. This is the meal we will have together before we each go back to our own homes and lives. At that point I will come up to consciousness and wake up.

I've described both **Night School and Night Shift** dreams to students, friends and family and all report having similar experiences. We also believe that these are true out of body experiences that occur under the guise of normal sleep. At those times, our spirits have the opportunity to break free of the body to learn new things and help others in need. If you are having these dreams, rest assured that your inner teachers and guardians have called you for a special opportunity.

Shared Dreaming

Have you ever dreamed of someone only to discover they were dreaming of you also? This is a fairly common dream phenomenon but because we are not always able to verify the shared dream, we dismiss them as wishful thinking. At times you will want to interpret the person in your dream as an aspect of you. Other times you will know beyond a doubt that you were interacting with an aspect of the other person. These dreams will have the look and feel of reality as described in the section on precognitive dreams. You may even have the experience of physically hearing the individual speak into your ear while in the dream state. There is always a feeling of a real encounter and a lingering feeling of connection. We are all one and we are all connected through the network known as the unified field or matrix.

Example: One evening after attending a conference with my oldest friend, we were talking about past life dream experiences. I began to relate a specific dream and past life recall of a time in England in which I died of consumption as an infant. My friend immediately exclaimed that she had the same recall. She was an older sister whose sibling died in the cradle and left her with a lonely childhood. She missed her sister throughout that life. We knew right away that we had been in the same place and shared the same experience. It was an amazing experience for the two of us to put the pieces together and have a shared realization in the same moment.

Dreams of the Deceased

Most of the time the person sharing the dream with you will be alive. In other dreams the person visiting will be someone who has died. The dream state is a perfect place for those who have crossed over to connect with us. It is much easier for loved ones to contact us when the conscious mind is asleep and the spirit is awake. Fear, anxiety and an overwhelming desire to make contact with a deceased person will choke off the desired contact. Most dream visits occur when least expected, and you may not even be aware that it has taken place until you wake up. These experiences always leave the dreamer knowing that their loved one isn't really gone. They have only changed from one state of being to another. It gives everyone the chance to connect in a loving space and be at peace with the transition. Often important information about family relationships, property or last wishes are communicated.

Example: One of my students had a visit from her deceased mother. Her mother explained why she should end a two-year old fight with her stepfather over money in a savings account. My student felt that her stepfather should distribute the funds to all the siblings. She was very angry when he held onto the money. In the dream, her mother explained that the money and the house were all he had to hold on to. My student and her siblings had their mother's love, their memories and the personal affects she gave them while alive. My student awoke with the understanding of her stepfather's motivation, and she could let go of her anger with him.

"I think we dream so we don't have to be apart for so long. If we're in each other's dreams, we can be together all the time."
A.A. Milne, *Winnie the Pooh*

Dreams of the Rich and Famous

If some celebrity shows up in your dream, they are most likely a symbol for something you believe or aspire to. They may also come from your subconscious reaching out to support that person. Many people have dreams of the President in which they are voicing their concerns or support for the decisions that have to be made in that office. Of course, some dreams of the rich and famous are simply fantasy, and there is absolutely nothing wrong with that.

Example: A friend of mine and I have a running joke that I'm quite the name dropper in my sleep state. I have had dreams with many celebrities throughout the years and some of them have been proven accurate with time. In one series of dreams, I found myself having dinner with a famous actor. I was listening to him bemoan his inability to have a long-lasting relationship. I listened to him for three nights, offering advice and acting as a sounding board. I assured him that love was in his future and marriage would follow. After the third night, I complained to my sister that I was tired of eating dinner with him. Later on, I learned that he and his current flame had parted ways. I was not surprised that he remained a bachelor for many years. I was also not surprised when I heard that he met and subsequently married his current wife. To this day they remain happily married.

Example: Another interesting dream was with a famous musician. In this dream I was taken to a white house by my guide who led me down a white hallway with many rooms. I was guided to sit at a table in one of these small rooms and wait for my client to arrive. When this musician sat before me, I knew I was there to help him. During our intuitive session, I advised him of the areas within self that needed to be addressed and healed. He confided in me that he was sick of the industry and didn't want to make music any more. He was tired of the scrutiny and people pulling and clamoring at him. He wanted peace. We talked for a while and I encouraged him not to abandon his music or his creativity. I told him that he would be making one more album and that it was important not only for him, but for his fans and those who would hear the music. Three months later I heard this musician announce that the group was going back into the studio to make an album after years without recording.

In both dreams, I had no desire to know either of these men personally and was not really a fan of either to a great degree. What I learned from these dreams was that the rich and famous have the same angst, fears and personal issues as the rest of us. They are much more limited in where they can turn for help. Shared dreams may lead to solutions to our problems when other avenues are not available.

Psychological or Local Dreams

In this book, *local dreaming* refers to present tense. These dreams usually revolve around recent past or current life experiences, and give us the opportunity to work through fears or issues. You can recognize them by their content and feel; they will most likely be centered on daily work or family situations. If we were dogs, these would be the dreams in which we chase that cat until we finally catch him.

Psychological dreams allow the mind to work out the stresses of the day or week and let you put them to rest. For most of us, they will be a rehashing of a work situation or an argument with the in-laws. In these dreams we find ourselves in a current situation, but given the opportunity to respond differently. The more focused we are on daily dramas of a mundane nature, the more these dreams will appear in our inner landscapes.

If most of your dreams fall into this category, you may want to consider that you are too focused on the very mundane aspects of life. Focus instead on resolving the lessons expressing themselves in your dreams. You can use the dream symbol interpretation learned earlier to decipher the deeper meaning your soul is trying to convey. Psychological dreams can also be recurring dreams until the lesson is integrated.

Expand your creative outlets to include a spiritual practice that takes you out of the daily grind. Go deeper and connect with your inner self to experience the greater universe. Taking a look at your life from the soul's perspective can help put daily life into balance.

Recurring Dreams

Recurring dreams are messages that we have unresolved issues, fears, karma or past life memories to look at. They can also alert you to opportunities coming your way so you'll be ready to accept them in waking life. It's as if your subconscious or spirit is trying to tell you to pay attention. The message is repeated over and over again using different scenarios to present the same truth. Once the conscious mind gets it, the dreams stop.

**"In the dream life you don't deliberately set out to dream about a house night after night; the dream itself insists you look at whatever is trying to come into visibility."
Jane Hirshfield, *The Atlantic Online,* Sep. 18, 1997**

Example: I had a client who had recurring dreams of being a knight at the king's court in England. In his dreams, he would meet and start a relationship with a skilled and beautiful woman. He described her as someone familiar with herbs and natural remedies who worked especially well with animals. She was someone of favor with the court and held a position of power due to her psychic abilities. She always looked the same in his dreams and he was completely infatuated with her. As a result, he was searching for her when I met him. I advised him to look at the dreams and ask what his soul was trying to convey to him. I cautioned him about his desire to possess this person in his current life, but he would not be dissuaded. She was what he wanted. Sometime later a mutual friend told me that he had met the woman of his dreams and she had isolated him from all his friends. He was under her control and working full time to pay for her many trips here and abroad. She was not working and he was too busy to stay in touch. I had no doubt that his recurring dreams had stopped.

For years I would periodically dream of going to my college post office to pick up an important piece of mail. In some of the dreams I would be unable to remember the combination, while in others, I couldn't find the building or I'd get lost on campus. At other times I would get to the post office and become distracted by trying to make a phone call to someone for an important reason. I couldn't get the call to connect or remember their phone number. I knew my soul was attempting to communicate an important message, but my fears and self-doubts were in the way.

Nightmares

Nightmares are an important indication of the fears we carry within. Whether our fears originate in this life or a past life makes no difference. They will continue to take shape in our dreams until they are faced and released. Children have nightmares more often than adults because they don't have the vocabulary to express their fears. Monsters will threaten their lives (instability at home) or scare them with unseen faces or shapes (fear of the unknown future). Rather than dismissing childhood nightmares, we should give children the tools they need to conquer their fears. Faith in a greater power, faith in their own inner strength and a strong self-esteem is a great place to start.

Example: When my young granddaughter told me she was being chased by a monster in her dreams, I told her to pull out her light sword and tell the monster, "I am the Light and you have to leave". I assured her that the monster had to follow her command. At first, she was a bit hesitant that she could do it, so I reminded her that her guardian angel, Lala, was always with her, even in her dreams. I'm happy to say that she was able to conquer her dream monsters and remain strong in the face of negative circumstances in her life during that time period.

"Dreams come to tell us something about our lives that we are missing."
-James Redfield, *The Celestine Prophecy*

Puns or humorous dreams

Sometimes the dream message can be conveyed with humor or a play on words. If you are a person who likes word games or puns, your dreams may be filled with them for you to ponder upon waking.

It's perfectly fine to wake up laughing or experience a belly laugh while dreaming. What a great way to receive a lesson or just release the stress of a full life. Every type of dream has a personal message if we are open to receiving it.

Example: A dream of ice skating on a warm, sunny day with a friend or relative may mean that you're skating on thin ice with that person. In that case, your soul is giving you a heads-up about your own behavior.

Record the Types of Dream Experiences You've Had:

Numbers and other dream symbols

Numbers in dreams can be taken literally. And people have won money doing just that. More often than not they are symbolic and open to interpretation.

Numbers appear in dreams all the time. A basic understanding of the meaning of numbers will certainly add another layer of depth to your dream interpretations. You may want to learn the deeper meanings of numbers through the study of numerology. For now, the chart below will give you a very basic set of meanings and a good starting point to expand your symbol vocabulary.

Quick List of Numbers and Their Meanings

Number 1: The masculine aspect or a male, leadership, trailblazing, new beginnings

Number 2: The feminine aspect or female, patience, duality, partnership, cooperation

Number 3: Expansion, growth, balance in mind, body, spirit, creativity, self-expression

Number 4: Making of plans, work, building, dependable foundations

Number 5: Testing or pushing boundaries, learning, travel, freedom, change

Number 6: Intuition, devotion, healing self and situations, harmonizing desires, marriage, family

Number 7: Hidden knowledge revealed, etheric forces, spirit over mundane pursuits

Number 8: Success and prosperity, responsible work, increased finances, achievement

Number 9: Tolerance, forgiveness, understanding, service to others, end of a cycle

Number 11: New beginnings, expansion of light into community, public service

Number 22: Divine love, intuitive expansion, your soul path

Example: A dream where the price of a car is $155 will alert the dreamer that they (#1) will want to break free (#5) of their current situation to achieve the freedom they desire (the second #5). It can also mean that there is a new project or life situation that will bring about inner tests and change in the person's life. The exact meaning of the numbers in the dream will depend on what your intuition tells you feels right and the circumstances of your life at the time.

Example: One of my students reported dreaming of starting a new business. He wasn't sure if the idea was worth pursuing and asked to have a dream that would provide insight and direction. My student dreamed that he was in a municipal building talking to a clerk at the counter. The clerk told him that the fee to register the name of the business was $4. My client took this to be a positive sign that the business would require work and would be the foundation of dependable business. He woke knowing that his idea was worth pursuing and would successfully provide for him and his family.

Astrology Symbols in Dreams

The symbolism of astrology has been with us since the beginning of time. Astrological symbols can populate our inner landscape, providing insights into situations. In astrology there are houses, planets and signs, and each bring something different to the dream. The context in which astrological symbols appear can let us know how they want to be interpreted.

A dream that includes a house number and street address may be pointing to astrological houses and their meanings. For those who have a background in astrology, there will be even more detail and deeper meaning in the house numbers and signs.

Meaning of the 12 Houses

1st House: The Self, how we look or face the outer world

2nd House: Money, material goods, financial matters, that which we value

3rd House: Communication, siblings and colleagues, schoolmates

4th House: Family, home, parents and childhood

5th House: Love, children, creativity and relationships

6th House: Daily life, work, health and habits

7th House: The Other, opposite of 1st house self - other people, marriage, contracts

8th House: Transformation, birth and death, finances, sexuality

9th House: Spirituality, distant travel, law, higher learning

10th House: Public persona, professional career, ambition, achievement

11th House: Friends, protectors and supporters, group activities

12th House: The unconscious mind, confinement, hospitals, prisons, solitude, self-sacrifice

Astrology Signs and Symbols

Aries the Ram: Strong sense of justice, ambitious, curious, optimistic, impatient, easily bored

Taurus the Bull: Dedicated, reliable, dependable, stubborn, dislike change

Gemini The Twins: Enjoy social situations, communicative, nervous, excitable

Cancer the Crab: Need to feel protected, strong connection to home and family, strong emotions

Leo the Lion: Loyal, charismatic, optimistic, outgoing, ego driven

Virgo The Virgin: Organized, analytical, intuitive, great story tellers, critical, especially of self

Scorpio The Scorpion: Focused, intense, secretive, hidden, confident, healer, intuitive

Sagittarius The Centaur: Explorer, scholar, love freedom, teacher

Capricorn The Goat: Intelligent, ambitious, purposeful, systematic, confident

Aquarius The Water Bearer: Unorthodox, humanitarian, remote, friendly, artistic, visionary

Pisces The Fish: Dreamer, honest, compassionate, introverted, gullible, psychic

As you can see from the list of astrology signs, animals can also be symbolic as they appear in dreams and life events. If you have crabs running around in your dream, it can mean a desire to be loved and appreciated by family. Crabs may also mean the inability to let go of a person or situation. You will need to use your own intuition and experiences to determine what it means for you.

Record Recurring Numbers and Astrology Symbols:

How to Improve Dream Recall

Whether you are hoping to get the answer to an important question, visit with loved ones or remember a precognitive experience, improving your dream recall is paramount. Whenever you are establishing a new habit, focused intent and diligence are required. Improving dream recall is no different. First let's cover the basics:

1. Don't expect dream recall when you are exhausted or on depressive medications. If your body is shut down due to extreme exhaustion or sluggish from prescription drugs or alcohol, dreaming will be difficult if it occurs at all. Drugs and chemicals can induce dreams filled with fear images bordering on hallucination. These dreams are confusing and more often than not should simply be interpreted to mean that your body is chemically unbalanced.

2. Expect to have dreams and expect to remember them. Before going to sleep, say: "I will remember the dreams I have tonight."

3. Be prepared to record your impressions, feelings or thoughts with as little physical movement as possible. Moving the body will engage the left brain and pull you out of dreaming consciousness. Students often report the dream images slipping away as they roll over or get up to record their dreams. One student said that when this happens to her, she gets back in bed in the same position in which she awoke. Her muscle memory would bring the dream details back into focus for her. Until you have good dream recall, I would recommend using your cell phone or a digital voice recorder kept on the night stand, so you can easily reach over and begin speaking.

4. Record something every day, even if it's just a feeling or impression. While establishing a new set of behaviors, it's important to be consistent. This will signal to your subconscious that you are committed to dream recall and will reinforce the new habit.

Here's a powerful 30-day method for improving dream recall taught by Dr. Mark Thurston in the early 1980's. It outlines a simple pre-bed routine that I've used and recommended over the years.

1. **15 Minutes in prayer** – This is where you talk to God or set your intention. Prayers of gratitude are encouraged.
2. **15 Minutes of Meditation** – This where we sit quietly and listen.
3. **Go to Sleep** – This 30-minute routine should be the last thing you do before laying down to sleep.

This method has never failed to improve dream recall if the student consistently followed this routine.

An Easy Method to Map Your Inner Landscape

Now that you have a new way identify and decode symbols, the next step is to organize your experiences into a journal.

1. Record your dream in your journal. Include all the details you can remember.
2. Write down your feelings and general thoughts about the dream.
3. Note the symbols in your dream and list them separately
4. Now add your interpretation of the symbols you've listed
5. Put your symbol interpretations in context of the overall dream to create a dream narrative

This method will help your mind organize the dream experience and provide a narrative for the message you are being given. Over time, you'll be able to read through your interpretations and see a beautiful story unfold – the story of your life!

You can apply this technique to your waking life as well. Look at recurring messages and symbols in your environment, and in the events that happen every day. Journal important events even if their meaning is not immediately clear. Using the steps outlined here will give you the tools to decipher the universe's important messages.

Record a Dream and Your Interpretation:

"A dream which is not interpreted is like a letter which is not read."
-The Talmud

In Summary

I encourage you to open a deeper dialogue with your Soul or Inner Guidance. Begin right now at whatever level of dream recall and interpretation you find yourself. Don't be afraid to dream and recall them. *Remember your dreams are you.* If you dream something ugly or frightening, it's most likely a fear that needs love, forgiveness, understanding and healing. Embrace those parts of yourself and allow them to heal, and your entire life will improve. If you dream of wonderful experiences, people and situations, those are also you. Embrace and enjoy them. Recognize the fantastic person you are and all the talents and gifts you bring to the world. Positive self-esteem is good thing.

Your consciousness will expand. New intuitive avenues will open up as you become better at listening to the language of the Soul. Your expanded ability will guide you to correct decisions and may one day save your life and the lives of those you love.

"Our dreams disturb us because they refuse to pander to our fondest notions of ourselves. The closer one looks, the more they seem to insist upon a challenging proposition: You must live truthfully. Right now. And always. Few forces in life present, with an equal sense of inevitability, the bare-knuckle facts of who we are, and the demands of what we might become."
-Marc Ian Barasch, *Healing Dreams*

Front and back cover artwork by
Mysticartdesign

48927502R00071

Made in the USA
Middletown, DE
16 June 2019